Prewriting: Strategies for Exploration and Discovery

CONSULTING EDITORS: **Gregory Cowan** and **Elisabeth McPherson,** FOREST PARK COMMUNITY COLLEGE

Random House, New York

Ray Kytle CENTRAL MICHIGAN UNIVERSITY

PREWRITING

Strategies for Exploration and Discovery

ISBN: 0-394-31542-1

Library of Congress Catalog Card Number: 76-161681

The first chapter incorporates, in slightly modified form, an article by the same
author entitled "Prewriting by Analysis" which was first published by the NCTE
in *College Composition and Communication* (December 1970), 380–385.

Manufactured in the United States of America
Composed by Cherry Hill Composition, Pennsauken, N.J.
Printed and bound by Halliday Lithograph, West Hanover, Mass.

First Edition

987654321

ACKNOWLEDGMENT IS GRATEFULLY MADE FOR PERMISSION TO REPRINT THE FOLLOWING:

Excerpt from Bonaro W. Overstreet, *Understanding Fear in Ourselves and
Others,* Copyright 1951 by Harper & Row, Publishers, Inc.

Excerpt from A. Delafield Smith, *The Right to Live.* Reprinted by permission
of the publisher, University of North Carolina Press.

Liza Williams, "Hippiebums," from "Flotsam and Jet Set," *Los Angeles Free
Press.* Reprinted by permission of Liza Williams through her agent Roslyn Targ
Literary Agency, Inc. Copyright © 1967 by Liza Williams.

Excerpt from Ashley Montagu, *Man: His First Two Million Years.* Copyright ©
1957, 1962, 1969 by Ashley Montagu. Originally published as *Man: His First
Million Years.* Reprinted by permission of the publishers, Dell Publishing Co., Inc.

FOR JAN

Preface

Getting started. That's the hard part. And the longer it takes—the more time spent staring at the blank page, or at the wall, or out the window—the more depressing the whole thing gets.

What a writer needs are some workable techniques for getting started, and for getting started right, so he doesn't have to stop part way through and then start all over again. In this book we are going to discuss and illustrate four effective ways of getting started: analysis, analogy, brainstorming, and systematic inquiry. These are four *prewriting* techniques.

Prewriting refers to what the writer does before he actually begins to write. Composition doesn't begin when you put pen to paper to write the first word of the first sentence of your essay or paragraph. Probably the most crucial aspect of composition comes before that moment. In this "before writing" (or "prewriting") stage the writer explores his subject, discovers his attitudes and opinions about it, and organizes his ideas into an effective order of presentation.

When you employ the prewriting methods discussed in this book, you will never find yourself staring at a blank page wondering "What do I want to say?" or thinking "I don't have anything to say." For you will have discovered *what* you want to say, *how* to say it, and the *order* in which to say it. Each of the four prewriting techniques culminates in a detailed, polished outline from which you can derive a precise and exact thesis statement.

For too long composition instructors and composition texts have focused on the product rather than on the process. They have described the characteristics of the effective essay rather than the process by which such an essay is composed. To my mind, this traditional approach has all the merits of trying to teach someone how to bake a delicious cake by describing the shape, size, texture, and taste of delicious cakes. Though a person so instructed may learn to recite the characteristics of a prize-winning cake, he is still no closer to being able to bake one himself.

My belief is that in writing, as in so many other activities, *the process is the product*. When you have completed the process, you have also created the product. Such is the hypothesis that sustains this book.

R.K.

vii

On Choosing a Subject

Just a note here, a brief admonition.

All of us, in casual conversation and bull sessions, talk of matters we really know little about. We throw out sweeping generalizations about complex matters; we make blanket judgments; we assert and pontificate. Fine. Conversation is an exploratory activity. Our views clash with the views of others, explanations are given, and new facts are learned. If a "fact" we've claimed is shown to be false, we can abandon it; if others give reasons why a view we've expressed is narrow or dubious, we can change it. That's what discussion and debate and argument are all about.

But when you *write*, the rules of the game change, and change drastically. When you write you become, whether you like it or not, a superior being, a sort of god. No matter what you're writing on, the very act of writing on it casts you in the role of an authority, of a competent and informed spokesman on the matter. And if gods fail, they are not treated very nicely. Think of Jacqueline Kennedy's fate when she married Onassis, of President Johnson's when he promised to win the war in Vietnam and didn't.

The primary principle of effective and responsible writing is:

KNOW YOUR SUBJECT!

It sounds simple, easy, obvious. But putting it into practice—that's the catch.

All of us carry around a sort of "memory bank" of received opinions, half-truths, and bits of information and misinformation. Each of our minds is like a computer into which there has been fed an endless stream of "information" every minute, hour, day, and year of our lives. But no meticulous computer programmer has been around to ensure that only accurate information gets recorded, and, when we are asked to state an opinion on a subject, the light least likely to flash in our minds is INSUFFICIENT DATA.

This light rarely flashes because we have "opinions" about almost any subject that is likely to come up. For example:

Democracy: "Good. I've lived in one all my life. I can write about that."

Communism: "Bad. Tyranny; international conspiracy; no freedom; exile to Siberia; Stalin; Great Purge. I can write on that."

Marijuana: "Drug. Leads to harder stuff. Used at pot parties and orgies. Long-haired freaks trip out on it. I can write on that."

I'm simplifying here, of course. But the pitfall is real and the point must be made. The fact that you have opinions about a particular subject doesn't necessarily mean that you are qualified to write about it. Express your opinions in informal conversation— yes. If they get shot full of holes, you've learned something and nobody thinks the less of you. But when you *write* about a subject your readers expect thoughtful and informed views. They expect accurate information and sound argument. And you have the responsibility of fulfilling these expectations. You're the teacher; the reader is your student. If your ideas are not thoughtful, if your facts are inaccurate or distorted, if your conclusions don't follow, then you are a god that failed and your reader may turn angrily against you.

This comes down to something very simple, really. When you write, choose a limited subject that you are truly knowledgeable about. For example: "Undemocratic Regulations in My Dorm" instead of "Democracy"; "The Life Style of Curt Richard, A Hippie" instead of "Hippies"; "The Process of Hitting Up" instead of "Drugs." Leave the big, general, abstract subjects to the few authorities who are qualified to write about them or to the multitude of scribblers who supply the prejudiced and the unwary with stereotypes and simplifications that substitute for thought.

Contents

one

prewriting by analysis

Principle

Consider the lowly gumdrop. If you were asked to describe a lemon gumdrop, you might say that it was small, round, yellow, hard and gritty, sweet smelling, and lemon-flavored. If so, whether consciously or unconsciously, you have *analyzed* the object.

When you analyze an object or a topic, you examine it from different *points of view*. You look at various aspects of it. In this case, the gumdrop was analyzed from six points of view:

I. Size
   A. Small
II. Shape
   A. Round
III. Color
   A. Yellow
IV. Texture
   A. Hard
   B. Gritty
V. Smell
   A. Sweet
VI. Taste
   A. Lemon-flavored

You can use this process of analysis to "get started" quickly and easily on just about any subject. First of all, use analysis to *explore* your subject.

I · Exploration Through Analysis

Look at your subject from as many points of view as possible. This will help you recognize the complexity of the subject and will reveal the necessity of limiting the scope of your discussion. When you analyze a subject, you carry on a conscious "conversation with yourself." You ask yourself questions and then answer them. The answers, which you should jot down in outline form, are the analysis. We can illustrate this process using the subject "drugs."

QUESTIONING VOICE (QV) : What are some different points of view from which one can look at "drugs"? What are some different aspects of "drugs"? How can the subject be broken down into parts?

ANSWERING VOICE (AV) : Well, I think of heroin and marijuana, for example. They're not the same.

QV: What's the difference?

AV: You can get strung out on heroin. Nobody gets strung out on grass.

QV: From what points of view are you looking at the subject, then?

AV: From the points of view of addictive and nonaddictive drugs.

I. Addictive drugs
   Heroin
II. Nonaddictive drugs
   Marijuana

QV: What are some other points of view from which you can look at the subject?

AV: What about speed? It's something else.

QV: What do you mean?

AV: Well, it's not like heroin, but it's bad news.

QV: In what way?

AV: A guy can really get strung out on it.

QV: How?

AV: He's afraid to come down.

QV: Why?

AV: Coming down is a bummer.

QV: Then how is it different from
    heroin?

AV: It gets you hung up. You're
    afraid to come down.

QV: Is it addictive, then?

AV: Yeah, but not like heroin.

QV: How, then?

AV: Heroin gets your body, speed
    gets your mind.

QV: From what points of view are
    you looking at "drugs" now?

AV: Physically addictive drugs
    compared to psychologically
    addictive drugs.

  I. Addictive drugs
    A. Physically addictive
      Heroin
    B. Psychologically addictive
      Speed
 II. Nonaddictive drugs
    Marijuana

II · Limitation

After you've explored your broad subject, you're ready to *limit* it. You're ready to select that particular aspect of your subject that you know the most about and are hence best qualified to write on. But don't stop too soon. Keep breaking down your subject, keep bringing up new points of view, until you have come down to an aspect of the subject that you really know, that you can write about with authority and accuracy. To illustrate:

QV: All right. What do you know
    the most about, heroin,
    speed, or marijuana?

AV: I know plenty about
    marijuana, but so does
    everybody else. I'm more
    interested in speed.

QV: O.K. Analyze it. What are
    some of the points of view
    from which one can look at

the subject "speed"?

AV: What is it? Some people don't even know what speed is.

QV: What point of view is that? Classify it.

AV: Definition.   I. Definition

QV: What's another aspect of the subject "speed"?

AV: How you get it. Where you make your connection.

QV: What point of view is that?

AV: Sources.

QV: What are the main sources?

AV: Doctors and dealers.   II. Sources
                                          A. Doctors
                                          B. Dealers

QV: What's another point of view?

AV: The effects of using it.

QV: What are they?

AV: You don't sleep much, you   III. Effects
don't eat much, you burn up   A. Loss of sleep
your mind.   B. Loss of appetite

QV: What's another aspect of   C. Destruction of brain cells
the subject?

AV: How you use it. How you   IV. Preparing a hit of speed
get ready to hit up.

QV: O.K. You've looked at "speed" from four different points of view. Which one do you know the most about?

AV: How you prepare a hit. I've watched lots of speed freaks.

III · Analyzing the Limited Subject

When you explore a general subject through analysis, you quickly realize that it is far too broad and complex to serve as the subject for an essay. Most people are simply ignorant about many aspects of a broad subject such as "drugs." And if they are well-informed, it would take a whole book to set down what they know. So, you should limit your subject. Keep analyzing until you come to some aspect that you really know about and that can be fully explained in your paper. In this case, the aspect is "preparing a hit of speed." Now you are ready to analyze the *limited subject*:

QV: What are some points of view from which you can look at the limited subject?

AV: One point of view is "materials needed." The stuff you need to prepare a hit.

QV: What are they?

AV: You need some speed, a fit, water, cotton, a spoon, and a source of heat—a match or a candle or a stove, for example.

QV: O.K. What's another point of view from which you can look at preparing a hit?

AV: How you do it. The process.

QV: What are the main steps in the process?

AV: Put some crystals in the spoon; draw water into the fit; mix water from the fit with the crystals in the spoon; heat the spoon until the speed dissolves; put the cotton in the mixture; put the point in the cotton and draw the speed into the fit.

In outline form the analysis of the limited subject looks like this:

PREPARING A HIT OF SPEED
_____

I. Materials Needed

   A. Speed

    B. A fit

    C. Water

    D. Cotton

    E. A spoon

    F. Heat

      1. Match

      2. Candle

      3. Stove

II. The Process

    A. Put some crystals in a spoon.

    B. Draw water into the fit.

    C. Mix water from the fit with the crystals in the spoon.

    D. Heat the spoon until the speed dissolves.

    E. Put the cotton into the mixture.

    F. Put the point in the cotton and draw the speed into the fit.

NOTE: A common misconception is that, when one writes, he writes "on" or "about" a subject. Maybe this misconception is perpetuated by the Miss Othmars of the world:

But whatever the source of this notion, it is false. You should never write "on" or "about" a subject because the result will be an unfocused and formless paper. Instead, you should elaborate, support, and illustrate particular and specific *assertions* about a subject. But before you can do so, you have to discover what you wish to assert. This—discovering what you wish to assert about your subject—is a primary function of analysis.

So, even when your subject appears quite limited, you should analyze it to determine what you want to say about it, and to order and structure your content.

Even if you start off with a limited subject such as "preparing a hit of speed" or "the life style of Curt Richards" or "dangerous side effects of the pill," you still need to analyze the subject before you begin to write. Analysis of the limited subject provides an order and structure for your composition. The major points of view from which you look at the limited subject become the main divisions in your paper. And such an analysis allows you to see where you are going, to see what you intend to say, and to formulate a topic sentence, or thesis, that reveals to the reader the scope and direction of your paper.

IV · Formulating Your Thesis

At this point, *after* you have analyzed the limited subject, you are ready to formulate your topic sentence or thesis statement. In this case you might write: "Preparing a hit of speed requires special materials and knowledge of how to use them." Your topic sentence or thesis is derived directly from the outline of your analysis, so you won't have any trouble clarifying it. If, on the other hand, you write out a general statement *before* analysis, it's easy to run into trouble. Say you took the subject "drugs" and started right out with a statement such as "Drugs are a big problem in America today." You've had it. Your essay is doomed from the start. For no matter what you say, you can't possibly cover your subject in the space and time available. "What drugs?" "All drugs?" "Prescription drugs?" "Over-the-counter drugs?" "Hard drugs?" "ALL hard drugs?" "What kind of problem?" "To whom?" "Why?" "How?" "Who says?" "How do you know?" You can't possibly answer all of the reader's legitimate questions in just a few pages, and many of them you're not really qualified to answer at all.

But if you use analysis to explore the broad subject, and then limit yourself to a small part of it that you are knowledgeable about, and then analyze that limited subject, you are on solid ground.

Process and Production

Student Process and Production

1

When you analyze a subject by looking at it from various points of view and classifying these points of view, you should embody the analysis in an OUTLINE. *In outlines the major points of view are indicated by Roman numerals, subdivisions of each major point of view are indicated by capital letters, and different aspects of the capital-letter subdivisions are indicated by arabic numerals.*

The student whose analysis and essay appear below chose "photography" as her general subject. She then analyzed her subject from three major points of view: taking the picture, developing the picture, and printing the picture.

PHOTOGRAPHY

I. Taking the picture
  A. Choice of camera
  B. Exposure
      1. Shutter speed
      2. Aperture size
  C. Composition
      1. Setting
      2. Lighting
      3. Purpose
II. Developing the picture
  A. Controls
      1. Temperature
      2. Time
      3. Agitation
  B. Procedure

III. Printing the picture
   A. Enlarger
   B. Printing paper
   C. Procedure

Her next step was to *limit* her subject and to analyze that limited subject. She chose to limit herself to subdivision A ("controls") under point of view II ("developing the picture"). When she analyzed this limited subject, she came up with this outline:

CONTROLS IN PICTURE DEVELOPMENT

  I. Temperature
    A. The lower the temperature, the longer the development time.
    B. Water and chemicals should be the same temperature.
 II. Time
    A. Recommendations by supplier are best guide.
    B. Excessive contrast can be eliminated by reducing development time.
III. Agitation
    A. What it is
    B. Necessary to prevent streaks
    C. Desirable amount of agitation

On the basis of this analysis of her limited subject, the student wrote the following theme.

Controls in Picture Development

Photography has long been a popular hobby. And with the technical advances in darkroom apparatus and chemicals that have been made in recent years, individual home darkrooms are on the increase. Although the procedure of developing and printing film is basically simple, much experience is necessary before one can consistently turn out good prints. Especially important is learning to control temperature, time, and agitation.

The first problem is temperature. Lower temperatures increase development time; thus, for best results, it is essential to have an accurate thermometer and knowledge of time and temperature correlations. Also, the closer the chemicals and water are to being the same temperature, the better the results will be. Too much variation causes grain in the negative.

Another important control is time. Recommendations supplied with the film or developer are the best guides. However, it should be remembered that these are not absolute rules; modifications are often necessary. If negatives consistently emerge too "contrasty," the development time should be cut by 20 to 30 percent because contrast, or the difference between highlights and shadows, increases with time. The longer the development time, the more silver is formed, which results in a blacker negative image.

Finally, there is the matter of agitation, the importance of which is often unrecognized by beginners. Agitation involves gently rocking the tank containing the film and developer in order to remove exhausted developer and to work fresh developer into the emulsion layer of the film. Agitation keeps the solution uniform, so that streaks don't occur. Agitation should begin as soon as the film is placed in the developer and should continue for ten to fifteen seconds. After that, agitation is usually advisable for about five seconds out of every minute of the remaining time. Over-agitating causes a lack of contrast.

Although film development is a relatively simple process, control of the three foregoing factors—temperature, time, and agitation—can mean the difference between a very good photograph and a very poor one. Before anyone can master the art of film development, he must first master these controls.

Notice that it took the student three hundred words to write an adequately developed essay on a subdivision of a subdivision of her original broad subject ("photography"). In writing you should shun the broad, unlimited subject. The more you limit, the more precise and specific you can be. And the more precise and specific you are, the better the reader will understand you, the more he will learn from your essay.

Student Production

Below is another student essay based on prewriting by analysis. Here the topic is more controversial, and the writer's intention is to convince as well as to inform. After you've read the essay, I'll ask you to explain how this writer analyzed and limited her subject.

Listening

Much of our modern literature and behavior give evidence of our concern with the lonely and separate estate of man—with his inability to establish deep and intimate relationships with others and with his frustration that he cannot make a real personal impact on the culture in which he lives. The growth of sensitivity sessions designed to help people relate better to others, the growing feeling (reflected by frequent commentaries in our media) that schools, religious groups, and political figures are unresponsive to the needs of the people they are intended to serve, and the growth of mass movements of protest against observable ills in our society—all these testify to the dissatisfaction and unrest felt by much of our population. Much of this very real and deep need is rooted in the fact that there is no one, apparently, who *hears*, no one who actively listens to what is being said. In "A Hard Rain's A-Gonna Fall," song writer Bob Dylan says: "Heard ten thousand whisperin' and nobody listenin'." The major function of the counselor, minister, or psychiatrist is often simply to listen. Hospital "crisis centers" are established to listen, to provide a link or a grip on the world for those whose loneliness and desperation drive them to apathy and despair. Telephone operators often are listening posts for those who have no one else. All these symptoms of man's isolation and of his frustrated need to communicate carry an important message for parents. Parents need to open and maintain the lines of communication in their own homes. They can

16

undercut the trend toward alienation and separation by listening to their children with a sympathetic ear.

Often, listening need be only superficial, as when a parent wishes to ascertain factual material like where his child is going (or has been) and what he is going to do (or has done). The parent has thus received important information, and the child has satisfied himself that his parent is interested in his life and has been willing to give him the spotlight, no matter how briefly. Too, parents may avert a crisis by listening at the right moment. Having a sympathetic ear into which to pour the anger and hostility built up by a sibling, by friends, by the weather, or by cancellation of an anticipated activity may well prevent a more serious outburst later. We all recognize the need to "blow off steam"; no one has more of this need than a child, who must be taught a safe way to rid himself of burdensome and potentially dangerous emotions.

There are times, however, when a parent needs to be aware of the meaning behind his child's words. When he greets an agitated child at lunchtime, he needs to dig below the story of "All the kids pick on Pat; they say he's retarded." Is it Pat he's talking about? Or is he asking "Am I? How do I know that I am not?" and pleading "Reassure me"? Fear and uncertainty caused by a recent death or sudden separation may lead to all kinds of seemingly irrelevant questions or even to strange silences. Parents must analyze the questions and listen to the silences for the important questions that lurk there, and these questions must be answered; reassurance of a very real nature has to be forthcoming.

Many subjects which children bring up are vehicles for measuring parental love. The child who reports with delighted horror on a misdeed (his or someone else's) may well be testing the basic regard his parents hold for him. He may be asking, "Would you still love me if I did this? Would you let me do this?" The stormy, tempestuous cry of "I never do anything right!" is a cry that calls for reassurance, to let the child know that parental love is not dependent on "proper" performance.

When Frank constantly recounts tales of Johnny's picaresque forays against the teacher and the neighborhood shopkeepers, then Frank's parents had better do a little serious listening. Perhaps Frank admires Johnny and is thinking of a little adventure of his own. Or Frank may want to be reassured, to know that Johnny's romantic peccadillos don't enhance him in adult eyes, that acceptable behavior is not dull and unrewarding. Or, he may even be describing his own activities. He may be asking his parents to wake up and apply the brakes, to help him to control himself.

Many of the apparently straightforward questions that children ask, as well as their comments on the passing scene, are really attempts to establish a system of values, to understand life, and to set up criteria for evaluating their own acts and those of others. When Johnny complains that the teacher disallowed gym for the whole class because a few children were misbehaving, he wants to be assured that his parents see the injustice in this action and that they hold justice to be a worthwhile aim. Because children and adolescents tend to see life in simplistic terms, Johnny doesn't want to discuss extenuating circumstances (this comes at a later age); he wants to know about the value itself—whether to hold it or to abandon it. Unless parents do listen to the plaints of their children, they can't hope to nurture in them a universal concern for justice, a feeling that all men should be treated fairly.

Thus, like the psychiatrist "listening with the third ear," parents must hear and respond to the questions and concerns that lie behind the words of their children. By doing so, they can demonstrate that words need not be weapons, that it is possible to talk to, rather than simply at, another.

Applications

1. The writer started out with the general subject "listening." Analyze this subject from at least four major points of view, including the point of view that this writer chose as her limited subject.
2. The writer chose "listening to our children" as her limited subject, and then analyzed that limited subject. State the four major points of view from which she looked at her limited subject and label them with Roman numerals.
3. What is the purpose of the rather long introductory paragraph? How does it make convincing the writer's statement that "Parents need to open and maintain the lines of communication in their own homes"?
4. What qualities or characteristics of this essay are most responsible for its effectiveness?

Published authors also use analysis to explore their subjects and to structure their essays. As you read the following selection, identify the broad subject, the aspect of the broad subject to which the author has limited himself, and the major points of view from which he examines his limited subject.

Why Our Fear-Problem Remains Unsolved
Bonaro W. Overstreet

Of all the emotional forces that pattern our individual and interpersonal behaviors, fear has the most insidious power to make us do what we ought not to do and leave undone what we ought to do. Under its influence, and trying to escape its influence, we seem fated to give it a yet stronger hold upon us.

This compounding of fear has gone on, we can assume, as long as man has been self-consciously man. It goes on also in most of our personal lives, so that these, as the years pass, often become less confident and free instead of more so. If, today, we live in a time of crisis, it is in large measure because the fear-born follies of our individual and group pasts have piled up in the present. Errors of omission and commission crowd us now, demanding of us a swift new wisdom about destructive fears and the conditions that foster them. To call a halt to this compounding of folly—or even to slow its progress—we must become clear about some of the reasons why we have not yet made any adequate attack upon our human fear-problem.

High among these reasons is the simple fact that we often fail to recognize fear for what it is. No other emotion wears so many disguises—convincing disguises that make us, time and again, treat it as something other than itself.

These disguises can best be understood as psychological forms of "protective coloration." We put them to work, however, in ways that are a travesty upon genuine self-defense. With them, we deceive not only our enemies but also those strangers and casual acquaintances who might become friends if we offered them any open lane of approach. We deceive those who love us and want to help us but who are invited by our "self-protective" behavior to treat us in ways that increase our isolation. Worst of all, we deceive ourselves—so that the selves we defend against all attack bear progressively less and less resemblance to the selves that other people experience when they are with us.

Fear, for example, may disguise itself as courage. We see this in the case of the adolescent driver who, with his car full of age-group companions, lets himself be prodded on to ever greater speed and risk—and even to such follies as taking both hands off the wheel. He acts in this manner not because he is brave but because his fear of seeming afraid is more commanding than his fear of injury. We may call him a dare-devil; but to respond to him aright, we must understand him in terms of what he, in the grip of adolescent social fears, *does not dare to do*. He does not dare to acknowledge fear or to suggest caution.

Or fear may disguise itself as snobbishness. Thus Mrs. Phelps, in Ralph Ingersoll's novel, *The Great Ones,* "snubbed a great many people simply because she had been trained to snub anyone of whom she was not sure." Few among the snubbed, in such a case, or among those who witness the snubbing, have been trained to penetrate Mrs. Phelps's disguise and to see her as a woman afraid. The vast majority of them will see her, rather, as a woman of such wealth and prestige that she can afford to ignore the common standards of give-and-take; and because they themselves are confused where issues of power are concerned, many of them will reward her recourse to "protective coloration" by envying her, trying to get into her good graces, and granting her an immunity that she needs only because she lacks self-confidence in all situations except those she has been taught to dominate.

Fear may disguise itself as ambition; or as humility, loyalty, self-sacrifice, or a missionary zeal in a good cause. It may disguise itself as bohemianism or as meticulous respectability; as contempt for social popularity or as a driving urge to be the life of the party. Sometimes it hides in an extreme of material self-indulgence, and again in asceticism. It expresses itself as racial and religious prejudice, as chauvinism, as chip-on-the-shoulder hostility, as a self-pitying sense of being unappreciated. Or, taking over the body for its own ends, it disguises itself as illness.

Such a recital of disguises may seem a sophistic exercise that takes all meaning out of the word *fear*. What it seriously points to, however, is a fact that we shall have to take into account time and again: namely, that the "emotional economy" of the fear-ridden person is a desperate one. It is desperate because it expresses his urgent need both to avoid seeing himself as he is and to avoid facing reality-situations that he does not feel competent to handle. A prime reason why many of the fears to which we should attend escape our attention, or move us to unfitting response, is that they come before us in one or another disguise.

One kind of wisdom that is now deeply called for is a wisdom of discrimination. We have to learn, with some measure of accuracy, when we are dealing with fear and when we are not. For if we fail to recognize it under its changing masks—treating it as strength, for example, or as goodness; as stinginess, conceit, or deliberate cruelty —we will mistreat it as fear. Also, when it is turned loose in society —in home, office, school, church, legislative body—fear produces different results from those produced by the qualities it imitates; and we need to be able to recognize the difference. Thus, fear disguised as agreement produces different results from those of genuine agreement; fear disguised as love produces different results from those produced by the kind of love that casts out fear. Until we develop some practical skill in making such distinctions, there is slight chance that we will reduce in number or intensity the fears that now dissipate our powers and distort our interpersonal relations.

Applications

1. What is the author's broad subject?
2. To what aspect of this broad subject does the author limit his discussion?
3. What are some other major aspects of the broad subject that the author chose not to discuss? In other words, what are some other major points of view from which the broad subject could be examined?

4. What are the major points of view from which the author chose to examine his *limited* subject?
5. How does paragraph 7 differ from the two preceding paragraphs?
6. How might it be argued that paragraph 7 is less convincing than the two preceding paragraphs? What does this suggest about the nature of convincing writing?

Writing Projects

A. Choose two broad subjects with which to practice prewriting by analysis. Assume that you are prewriting a four- to five-hundred-word essay, and follow these steps:
   1. Explore the broad subject through analysis.
   2. Limit the subject.
   3. Analyze the limited subject.
   4. Embody your analysis of the limited subject in an outline.
   5. Formulate a thesis statement based on your outline of the analysis.
B. Choose the analysis you are most satisfied with and write a four- to five-hundred-word theme based on it.

two

prewriting by analogy

Principle

An *analogy* is an extended comparison between two unlike subjects. Analogies can be used to *argue a point*, to *clarify* or to *explore a subject*.

The Argumentative Analogy

An analogy compares two unlike subjects by discussing their similarities. But when a writer moves from pointing out similarities to implying that the two subjects are identical, he has committed the logical fallacy of *argument from analogy*. For example:

> The nervous system is very much the same as a telephone system. The central office is the brain, the nerves are the wires, and each cell in the body is a telephone user. If all the wires from the central office came out at one point as a cable, it would be as the spinal cord which is made up of billions of nerves which serve the same purpose as wires carrying messages to and from the brain.
>
> The brain controls all the activities of the cells through this network of wires. Irritation of these nerves by pressure from vertebrae slipping out of place would produce somewhat the same results in the body as a short or "crossed wires" in a telephone system.
>
> A person with such a condition would be known as a highly nervous wreck with symptoms far and many, such as tired feelings, sleeplessness, loss of appetite, highly irritable [*sic*], fidgety [*sic*], hallucinations, digestive disturbances etc., and might lead to a nervous breakdown.
>
> Chiropractors are as highly specialized linemen who ferret out these "shorts" and adjust them with the result that normal service is resumed.*

In the first part of the analogy above, the writer points out similarities between the nervous system and a telephone system. Fine. But he then goes on to assert that the human nervous system, like a telephone system, can be "repaired" by finding and eliminating

---

* Quoted in Wallace L. Anderson and Norman C. Stageberg, *Introductory Readings on Language*, rev. ed. (New York: Holt, Rinehart and Winston, 1967), pp. 522–523.

"shorts." This conclusion follows only if the two systems are not different in any significant ways—but they *are* significantly different. The author is arguing from analogy, and his conclusion does not follow.

The Clarifying Analogy

The clarifying analogy explains and clarifies the unfamiliar by comparing it to something common and familiar. It says, in effect, "You will be better able to understand the unfamiliar subject I'm talking about if you think of it in terms of this familiar subject." For example:

Imagine that we stand on any ordinary seaside pier, and watch the waves rolling in and striking against the iron columns of the pier. Large waves pay very little attention to the columns—they divide right and left and re-unite after passing each column, much as a regiment of soldiers would if a tree stood in their road; it is almost as though the columns had not been there. But the short waves and ripples find the columns of the pier a much more formidable obstacle. When the short waves impinge on the columns, they are reflected back and spread as new ripples in all directions. To use the technical term, they are "scattered." The obstacle provided by the iron columns hardly affects the long waves at all, but scatters the short ripples.

We have been watching a sort of working model of the way in which sunlight struggles through the earth's atmosphere. Between us on earth and outer space the atmosphere interposes innumerable obstacles in the form of molecules of air, tiny droplets of water, and small particles of dust. These are represented by the columns of the pier.

The waves of the sea represent the sunlight. We know that sunlight is a blend of lights of many colours—as we can prove for ourselves by passing it through a prism, or even through a jug of water, or as Nature demonstrates to us when she passes it through the raindrops of a summer shower and produces a rainbow. We also know that light consists of waves, and that the different colours of light are produced by waves of different lengths, red light by long waves and blue light by short waves. The mixture of waves which constitutes sunlight has to struggle through the obstacles it meets in the atmosphere, just as the mixture of waves at the seaside has to struggle past the columns of the pier. And these obstacles treat the light-waves much as the columns of the pier treat the sea-waves. The long waves which constitute red light are hardly affected, but the short waves which constitute blue light are scattered in all directions.

Thus, the different constituents of sunlight are treated in different ways as they struggle through the earth's atmosphere. A wave of blue light may be scattered by a dust particle, and turned out of its course. After a time a second dust particle again turns it out of its course, and so on, until finally it enters our eyes by a path as zigzag as that of a flash of lightning. Consequently the blue waves of the sunlight enter our eyes from all directions. And that is why the sky looks blue.*

In the passage above the unfamiliar subject, the scattering of short light waves by dust particles, is clarified by comparison to the scattering of ripples by the columns of a pier.

The Exploratory Analogy

The exploratory analogy is, in a sense, a working hypothesis. It is a means of generating fresh insights and discovering new perspectives. By postulating similarities between two apparently disparate subjects, it leads to the perception of patterns and relationships. This section explains how the exploratory analogy can be used as a prewriting strategy.

I · Exploration Through Analogy

First of all, jot down a subject that you are knowledgeable about. This is your *primary subject.* Let's take "high school" for our first illustration, since we have all had plenty of experience with high school.

The next step is to cast around for an *analogous subject.* This should be some quite different sort of subject that reflects your attitude toward (or is suggested by) your primary subject—in this case "high school." Among the many possibilities, you might come up with "assembly line" or "jungle" or "jail." Let's work with "jail."

Once again you carry on a conversation with yourself, an "interior dialogue":

QV: So, being in high school was like being in jail?
AV: Damned right.
QV: O.K. What are all the characteristics of "jail" that you can think of?

* Sir James Jeans, *The Stars in Their Courses* (New York: Cambridge University Press, 1931).

AV: You're locked up. You're observed all the time. You get punished for slight infractions of the rules. There are lots of rules governing just about all your activities.

QV: What else?

AV: Guards are all over the place. If you give them any trouble, you get punished. You've got to behave and be respectful.

QV: What else?

AV: Let me think. . . . You have to serve a sentence; you're "in the cooler" for a certain length of time and can't get out sooner.

QV: What else?

AV: You get mad. You feel helpless. If you break out and get caught, you get sent back.

QV: Anything else?

AV: You spend your time in a cell with other prisoners.

QV: And?

AV: There's a fixed routine; at certain times each day you eat, you shower, you exercise. If you want to break with the routine, you have to get special permission.

This is how you proceed. Discover and list as many characteristics of the analogous subject as you can. In this case, we came up with these:

J A I L
_____

1. You're locked up.
2. You're observed all the time.
3. You get punished for violating rules.
4. Rules govern most activities.
5. Guards are all around.
6. If you give the guards trouble, you get punished.
7. You have to behave and be respectful.
8. You have to stay in jail until you've served your time.
9. You get mad.
10. You feel helpless.
11. If you break out and get caught, you get sent back.
12. You spend your time in a cell with other prisoners.
13. You live by a fixed routine.
14. If you want to break the routine, you have to get special permission.

The next step is to pair off each item in your list with an equivalent item for the primary subject. Don't force parallels, or you will turn off your reader. Just scratch out those items in your list that don't "transfer." After all, you're not trying to show that your high school *was* a jail. That's obviously false. Your point is that in many ways your high school *resembled* a jail, was *similar* to a jail.

JAIL	HIGH SCHOOL
You're locked up.	——
You're observed all the time.	Teachers and hall guards keep you under constant observation.
You get punished for violating rules.	You get punished for violating rules.
Rules govern most activities.	Rules govern most activities.
Guards are all around.	Teachers are all around.
If you give the guards trouble, you get punished.	If you give the teachers trouble, you get punished.
You have to behave and be respectful.	You have to behave and be respectful.
You have to stay in jail until you've served your time.	You have to stay in school until you're sixteen.
You get mad.	You get mad.
You feel helpless.	You feel helpless.
If you break out and get caught, you get sent back.	If you skip school and get caught, you get sent back.
You spend your time in a cell with other prisoners.	You spend your time in a classroom with other student "prisoners."
You live by a fixed routine.	You live by a fixed routine.
If you want to break with the routine, you have to get special permission.	If you want to break with the routine, you have to get special permission.

II · Selecting and Ordering

At this point we have a lot of ideas, but not much order. If we started writing now, we would produce a formless ramble.

It's important to realize that you don't need to say *everything* you know about your subject. That's writing *about* a subject, and we've already discussed the pitfalls of such an approach. What you need to do now is to come up with several *major* ways in which, to your mind, being in high school resembles being in jail.

An effective rule of thumb is provided by the proverbial challenge "Give me three good reasons." Of course you can give more than that, but three good reasons, fully explained and illustrated, will probably convince your reader.

Hence, after you have listed all the parallels between your primary subject (high school) and the analogous subject (jail), you should determine the major areas of resemblance between the two. To do this, you use the method of *classification*. When we discussed prewriting through analysis, we noted that you explore your subject by looking at it from different points of view. A point of view can always be labeled. In other words, you can indicate it by some classification. Hence, we first looked at drugs from the points of view (or classifications) of "addictive" and "nonaddictive" drugs. Later we reclassified drugs into three categories, "physically addictive," "psychologically addictive," and "nonaddictive." Classifying is a way of creating order. It establishes definite groups; it creates clear perspectives from which to examine a topic.

Thus, one way to determine the major areas of resemblance is to go through your list and put a classification word after each item. For our example, we would have:

ITEM	CLASSIFICATION
Teachers and hall guards keep you under constant observation.	Teachers
You get punished for violating rules.	Rules
Rules govern most activities.	Rules
Teachers are all around.	Teachers
If you give the teachers trouble, you get punished.	Teachers

I T E M	C L A S S I F I C A T I O N
You have to behave and be respectful.	Behavior
You have to stay in school until you're sixteen.	Sentence
You get mad.	Emotion
You feel helpless.	Emotion
If you skip school and get caught, you get sent back.	Sentence
You spend your time in a classroom with other student "prisoners."	Place
You live by a fixed routine.	Routine
If you want to break with the routine, you have to get special permission.	Routine

This classification reveals that the major areas of similarity are between:

    I. The role of teachers and the role of guards
   II. Rules in a high school and regulations in a jail
 III. Emotions of students and emotions of prisoners
 IV. Routine in high school and routine in jail
   V. Compulsory attendance in high school and a prisoner's jail sentence

Those classifications that appear only once—in this case "behavior" and "place"—can be dropped in order to achieve a more tightly focused paper. Similarly, before you move on to an outline, you should review your list of major areas of resemblance and cut out any that seem farfetched or "stretching the point." In the outline below, the idea that compulsory attendance for the student is like a prisoner's jail sentence has been omitted. The differences are so glaring that the comparison lacks credibility.

III · Outlining

You are now ready to make a preliminary sentence outline. As you construct the outline, you should search for additional parallels and include them.

I. Teachers in high school are like guards in a jail.
  A. They keep you under constant observation.
  B. They are all around.
  C. They punish you for disobedience.
  D. They enforce regulations.

II. Students in high school, like prisoners in a jail, are governed by elaborate rules.
  A. Rules govern most activities.
  B. You are punished if you violate rules.

III. Like prisoners in a jail, students feel caged.
  A. They get mad.
  B. They feel helpless.

IV. As in a jail, life in high school is controlled by a strict and inflexible routine.
  A. You live by a strict routine.
  B. If you want to break with the routine, you have to get special permission.

After you have constructed a preliminary sentence outline, you can perceive the overall structure and purpose of your argument. However, you will probably want to do some rearranging before phrasing your thesis. For example, in the preliminary sentence outline above, three items strike me as out of place—I B, I C, and III A. Item I B, "They are all around," is more general than the other items under Roman numeral I and should probably be either first or last. I prefer to put it first, having the discussion move from general to specific. Item I C, "They punish you for disobedience," is one way that teachers enforce regulations (I D), and should, therefore, follow I D. Item III A, "They get mad," is more emphatic and striking than III B, "They feel helpless," so to avoid a letdown, the order of A and B should be reversed.

I. Teachers in high school are like guards in a jail.
  A. They are all around.
  B. They keep you under constant observation.
  C. They enforce regulations.

D. They punish you for disobedience.

II. Students in high school, like prisoners in a jail, are governed by elaborate rules.
  A. Rules govern most activities.
  B. You are punished if you violate rules.

III. Like prisoners in a jail, students feel caged.
  A. They feel helpless.
  B. They get mad.

IV. As in a jail, life in high school is dominated by a strict and inflexible routine.
  A. You live by a strict routine.
  B. If you want to break with the routine, you have to get special permission.

After you have straightened out the order of the items under each Roman numeral, you should take a look at the order of the Roman-numeral points of view themselves. You can order them, for example, on the basis of cause-effect, least important–most important, first in time–last in time, problem-solution, general-specific, specific-general, comparison-contrast, or combinations of these and other principles of order. What's important is to have a clearly conceived reason for the order you choose, and to make your order clear to the reader by using appropriate transitions as you move from one major point of view to another.

In the revised sentence outline above, Roman numeral III seems out of place. I and II refer to similarities between jail life and school life; so does IV. Roman numeral III differs from the others because it not only points out a similarity, but also indicates the *results* of school being jaillike: helplessness and anger. Hence, I, II, and IV stand in a cause-effect relation to III. Using, then, a cause-effect order, we would come up with this revision:

FINAL SENTENCE OUTLINE

I. Teachers in high school are like guards in a jail.
  A. They are all around.
  B. They keep you under constant observation.
  C. They enforce regulations.
  D. They punish you for disobedience.

II. Students in high school, like prisoners in a jail, are governed by elaborate rules.
   A. Rules govern most activities.
   B. You are punished if you violate rules.
III. As in a jail, life in high school is dominated by a strict and inflexible routine.
   A. You live by a strict routine.
   B. If you want to break with the routine, you have to get special permission.
IV. Like prisoners in a jail, students feel caged.
   A. They feel helpless.
   B. They get mad.

IV · Formulating Your Thesis

You are now ready to phrase your thesis statement. The purpose of your thesis is to inform the reader of the main point of your essay. In this case, your main point is: "Many high schools are like jails." This sentence could be your thesis.

If you wish to give your reader a more detailed map of your essay, you can state the major reasons that support your thesis and the order in which you are going to present them. Such a "summary thesis" might read: "Many high schools are like jails. Teachers function like guards. Students, like prisoners, are governed by elaborate rules. And school life, like jail life, is dominated by a strict and inflexible routine. The result is that many students feel, like prisoners in a jail, helplessly and maddeningly caged in."

V · Supplying the Specifics

You are now ready to begin writing the first draft of your essay. As you compose this draft, be sure to supply specific examples and illustrations for each general statement you make.

Your reader is reasonable, but he isn't gullible. Your reader is willing to be persuaded, but he isn't about to accept your pronouncements on faith. His attitude is "Oh, yeah? Prove it!" If you don't "prove it," you won't convince him. And if you don't convince him, you've wasted your time and his.

To convince your reader, tell him about the specific instances and experiences that led you to form the opinion you are advancing. For if certain concrete experiences led you to certain conclusions, you can usually lead your reader to the same conclusions by sharing these experiences with him.

NOTE: When you explore a subject through analogy, you are deliberately searching for suggestive similarities between two subjects that are essentially *dis*similar. Analogy is not identity. The feelings of helplessness and anger that students in high school may experience are *not* the same feelings of helplessness and anger that prisoners in a jail experience. The former are "caged" only metaphorically, whereas the latters' "cage" is quite literally of stone and steel. Never lose sight of the "as if" or "like" quality of analogy; never take yourself too literally. For analogy suggests similarities only.

Process and Production

Student Process and Production

1

The student whose prewriting activities and essay appear below wanted to explore the plight of the aged in America. He chose as his subject "old people in America." When he cast around for a concrete image that would suggest a common attitude toward old people, the image of a scarecrow occurred to him. He decided to explore his subject by:

A. listing all the characteristics of scarecrows that might suggest qualities of his primary subject—old people in America
B. pairing off those characteristics of scarecrows with their primary subject equivalents, and
C. determining the major areas of similarity through the use of classification words.

A: Listing Characteristics of Scarecrows

1. They are ugly.
2. They seem somehow pathetic.
3. They seem lonely, alone, forlorn.
4. They scare birds.
5. They keep birds from eating grain.
6. They seem unfriendly.
7. They are cold, bloodless.
8. They aren't worth much.
9. They can be easily replaced.
10. They are ignored.
11. No one pays much attention to them.
12. They don't have friends.

13. They stay rooted in one place.
14. They are vaguely frightening.
15. I wouldn't want to touch one.
16. They're dirty and icky.

B and C: Developing the Analogy

SCARECROWS	OLD PEOPLE	CLASSIFI-CATION
They are ugly.	They are often regarded as ugly.	Ugly
They seem somehow pathetic.	They often seem pathetic.	Pathetic
They seem lonely, alone, forlorn.	They often appear lonely, alone, forlorn.	Lonely
They scare birds.	They often scare young people.	Scary
They keep birds from eating grain.	They often seem antagonistic to young people enjoying themselves.	Mean
They seem unfriendly.	They seem un-friendly (tight lips, frowning expression).	Unfriendly
They are cold, bloodless.	They seem dried up, withered.	Ugly
They aren't worth much.	They are often poor.	Worthless
They can be easily replaced.	Few people seem to think they matter.	Worthless
They are ignored.	They are ignored.	Ignored
No one pays much attention to them.	No one pays much attention to them.	Ignored
They don't have friends.	They often seem to have no friends, no	Lonely

SCARECROWS	OLD PEOPLE	CLASSIFI-CATION
	one who cares about them.	
They stay rooted in one place.	They aren't very active; they don't get around much.	Sedentary
They are vaguely frightening.	They are somehow a little frightening.	Scary
I wouldn't want to touch one.	I wouldn't want to touch one; they seem a little repulsive.	Ugly
They are dirty, icky.	They often seem vaguely "dirty"; they have old, dry, scaly skin.	Ugly

Selecting and Combining

When the student examined his classifications, he found that the major ways in which old people in America resemble scarecrows are these:

1. They are ugly (classification appeared four times).
2. They are lonely (classification appeared two times).
3. They are scary (classification appeared two times).
4. They are worthless (classification appeared two times).
5. They are ignored (classification appeared two times).

The student concluded that the apparent meanness and unfriendliness of old people were two additional reasons why they often seemed scary and decided to include these two characteristics in the "scary" classification. He also concluded that our tendency to ignore the aged increases their loneliness, and integrated this category with the "lonely" classification.

Ordering

The student's next step was to order his four major classifications. After studying them carefully, he decided that they could be arranged to reflect a cause-effect sequence. He decided that the *ugliness* of most old people—as judged by a youth-oriented society—was what made them particularly *scary* and that, as a result, they tended to be *lonely* and regarded as essentially *worthless*.

Outlining

After deciding the order in which he wished to discuss the similarities between scarecrows and aged people in America, the student constructed the following outline:

OLD PEOPLE AS SCARECROWS

I. Like scarecrows, old people are ugly.
   A. They are dried up and withered.
   B. They seem vaguely "dirty" with their old, dry, scaly skin.
   C. They strike one as repulsive to touch.
II. This physical ugliness makes them scary.
   A. They seem unfriendly, with their tight, thin lips and frowning expressions.
   B. They seem to resent youth for its pleasures and beauty.
   C. They remind us of what will be our fate.
III. Like a scarecrow isolated in a field, they seem lonely.
   A. They seem to have no friends, no one who cares about them.
   B. They seem forlorn.
   C. They are ignored, passed by, side-stepped.
      1. No one heeds them.
      2. People look away.
IV. They are regarded as worthless.
   A. They are often poor.
   B. Few people seem to think they matter.

Formulating the Thesis

Whatever prewriting method you use, you should not formulate your thesis until *after* exploration, limitation, and ordering. To form a thesis before these steps have been taken represents not perception but preconception. Hasty formulation of a thesis makes a wide-ranging exploration of a subject impossible, and such exploration is one of the objects of prewriting.

After you have explored and limited your subject, and after you have structured your discoveries in outline form, you can derive a precise and exact thesis directly from your outline, as the second sentence of the following essay illustrates:

The Aged as Scarecrows

In a youth-centered culture such as ours, which seems to value the body's beauty above almost all else, there is seldom dignity in old age. To be old is to be ugly, to be ugly is to be scary, and to be both ugly and scary is to be lonely.

Old people in our society are often accorded all the respect and dignity of scarecrows. For they have committed the unpardonable sin of the Pepsi Generation; they have become ugly. They appear dried up and withered. Many seem vaguely "dirty" with their old, dry, scaly skin. They are not "embraceable" and strike us as repulsive to touch.

This physical ugliness makes old people scary. Many seem unfriendly, with their tight, thin lips and their perpetually frowning expressions. They often seem to resent youth for its sensual pleasures and beauty. But, perhaps most frighteningly, they remind us of what we must someday be, but long never to be. They mirror our own inevitable future, and we turn away in fright and defensive aversion.

As a result, most old people in America are doomed to loneliness. With many of their own friends dead or scattered, they can expect no new ones from the young they repulse. We view them as scarecrows standing alone in a field. Their forlornness evokes no desire to approach, no human sympathy. Rather, they are ignored, passed by, side-stepped. Loneliness is simply their fate. To touch them is to be infected, and that, above all, must be avoided. To recognize their plight is to accept our eventual sharing of it, and that is too frightening for contemplation.

Ugly, scary, and lonely, the aged in America are often treated as if they were essentially worthless. In a society that values material success, they are often poor. Social security and, perhaps, a small annuity do not substitute for a well-paying job. Their inability to spend much money is grotesquely paralleled by society's unwillingness to spend much money on them or devote much attention to them. In our culture the aged are often regarded as human scarecrows.

Professional Production

The essay that follows was written by two professors to illustrate "the use of an analogy both for the conception of an idea and for its articulation." *

Strategy and Tactics in Writing · Gordon D. Rohman and Albert O. Wlecke

Military men divide the art of war into strategy and tactics. Generals take care of the former; sergeants the latter. Strategy involves the whole field of operations; tactics the specific field of the foxhole and the soldier. Strategy disposes of armies; tactics of squads. Strategy wins wars; tactics win battles.

The art of writing is analogous. Strategy here involves the large-scale planning and directing to insure that the idea gets stated,

---

* Gordon D. Rohman and Albert O. Wlecke, *Pre-writing: The Construction and Application of Models for Concept Formation in Writing* (Washington, D.C.: Cooperative Research Program, Office of Education, 1964), p. 70.

developed, compared and contrasted with skill; the intelligence to adjust the means to the ends of the composition desired and the audience imagined; the maneuvering of large bodies of proof and demonstration to support the offensive drive of the major idea; the mopping up of all possible objections to the idea in summation; and, finally, the setting of peace terms in conclusion. Strategy in writing means, in other words, defining a subject and assembling materials in relation to it. Defining a subject is not simply saying, "I think I'll write about American politics," or "I think I'll write about nature," any more than a general can simply yell "Charge!" The strategy of wars (Hannibal crossing the Alps, Eisenhower crossing the Channel), and the strategy of composition ("Roosevelt Packs the Supreme Court," *Walden*), need specific ends. From the vague and generalized aspiration, the good general and the good writer move to the precisely defined and limited objective. Failing in the specialization, neither can assemble forces to get the war won, the composition written: Hannibal needed elephants, Eisenhower landing craft. In addition, the general or the writer, to be strategically effective, must single-mindedly fix his attention upon the object of his campaign. Neither Hannibal nor Eisenhower could have triumphed without singleness of purpose. The subject, when finally defined, is really the subject as seen by a writer's particular way of regarding it; the war, when finally understood, is really the enemy as held by the general's particular way of engaging him.

Strategy concerns planning, tactics concern procedure within the broad decisions laid down by the general staff. Tactics in writing include such things as what to begin with, what to end with, what level of usage to employ, what sorts of proof to marshal, what kind of wit to employ, and, of course, what degree of "correctness" to insist on. Tactics in military maneuvers are full of short charges and withdrawals, digging in, enveloping a position by flank attack, hurrying up and waiting, boldness and caution, planning and guessing. The tactics of writing also involve drafting and redrafting, writing and erasing, checking and rechecking, hurrying through an inspired insight, and waiting for the cool detachment of criticism, witty maneuvers of metaphor, bold envelopment of analogies, and a good deal of plain marching of sentences in good order.

We contend that good writing is good strategy first and foremost. The wholeness of the whole composition we must first secure or all is lost; poor strategy loses wars, poor tactics only battles. Too often we are concerned only with the tactics of "correct" grammar, too seldom with the strategy of good design in writing. While we fuss with formalities, we lose the war. Sentences in Class A uniforms, Fowlered, Perrined, and Webstered, gallop off to annihilation like Tennyson's Six Hundred. The art of war is strategy first, tactics second. The art of writing cannot improve on this wisdom.

Applications

1. What is the primary subject, the subject the authors wish to explore?
2. What is the analogous subject, the "unlike" subject which enables the authors to "conceive and articulate" their views about the primary subject?
3. The authors limit themselves to two major aspects of the analogous subject. What are these two major aspects?
4. Indicate the two aspects of the primary subject which are discussed in terms of the two equivalent aspects of the analogous subject. (Indicate each with a single word) :

   ANALOGOUS SUBJECT   PRIMARY SUBJECT

   _____   _____

   _____   _____

5. Has this book concentrated on teaching you good *strategy* or good *tactics*?

Professional Production

In the preceding essay, "Strategy and Tactics in Writing," the analogy is quite explicit. The authors discuss the nature of strategy and tactics in war, and then explicitly compare them with their counterparts in writing; they keep the two sides of the analogy constantly before the reader.

Another approach is to explain first one side of the analogy, and then the other. In this selection from The Right to Live, *the author first discusses the functions of rules in a game. He then compares the way rules function in a game to the way laws function in society.*

Law as the Means to Freedom · A. Delafield Smith

We need to see what the true meaning and function of law is, not in terms of authority, which is so commonly mistaken for law, but in terms of the rule of law in the ideal sense as a guide and challenge to the human will.

The best example of how law, in the ideal sense, works, how it evokes the sense of freedom and stimulates the individual is the survey of a game. Have you ever asked yourself why the participation in a game is so excellent a medium for self-expression and character development? This question is often superficially answered in terms of the rein given to the competitive instincts of the individual and his "zest" for conquest. But have you ever considered that here, in a game, and perhaps here alone, we human beings really do act almost completely under the aegis of law? That, rather than competition, is the real source of the game's restorative value for the human spirit. Analyze the process step by step and you must be convinced that this is the truth.

Your first step upon entering a game is the assumption of a distinct personality. You become clothed in a personality defined by the rules of the game. You assume a legal or game personality. You may describe yourself as a first baseman, as a right guard, or as a dealer. But however you describe yourself you will see that what you have described is a legal status—one of the focal points in a legal pattern with rights and obligations suitable to the position. These rights and duties are defined by the rules under whose empery you have thus put both yourself and all others with whom you have dealings. Your status, your rights, your obligations, all are secure for the rules of the game are almost sure to be followed. The game indeed is defined by its rules. These are purely abstract. They are wholly free of will and dictation. They are pure rules of action composed usually in some physical setting which they serve to interpret and fashion till it becomes an arena of human action, just as, for example, the rules of the highway, in relation to the highway pattern itself, provide individuals with an arena on which they can operate successfully. Now the rules of the game have many functions. They, in fact, define the very goals that the players seek. One wins only in the context of the rules of the game. They determine inexorably the consequences of the player's action, every play that he makes. He acts solely in relation to the rules. Their empery is accepted like a fact or a circumstance. Finally, they challenge and stimulate him for he uses the rules to win. The game is otherwise unmanaged. An umpire or a referee is but an interpreter of the rules. He *can* be wrong. Such is the conception. This, then, may furnish an introduction to the real function of law in society.

Law gave birth to the concept of freedom. True it is that you can have no security in a situation in which every person and everything around you acts capriciously, unpredictably, or, in other words, lawlessly; but the point I wish to make is that while you would have no security in such an environment, it is more significant that you would have no freedom in such an environment. The reason you could not be free in such a situation is that you could not get anywhere you wanted to go or successfully do anything you wanted to do. You could make no plan in the expectation of carrying it out. You cannot possibly carry out any aim or goal of your own unless you have some basis for calculating what results may follow from any given act or activity of your own. Unless you can determine in advance what are the prospects and limitations of a given course of behavior, you cannot act intelligently. Whatever intelligence you may have will do you no good. You cannot adjust your own step to anyone else's step nor can you relate your conduct to any series of events or occurrences outside yourself except to the extent that they follow a pattern that you can learn about in advance of your action.

The only way to promote freedom is to devise a set of rules and thus construct a pattern which the various members of that society can follow. Each can then determine his own acts in the light of his knowledge of the rules. On this basis each can predict his field of action in advance and what results are likely to ensue from his acts; and so he gains freedom to plan and to carry out his plans. The more you attempt to administer society, however, the less free it becomes. There is opportunity for freedom of choice only in acting subject to the rules, and then only if the rules are freed of any element of will or dictation. If these rules are just rules that tell you what method or act will yield what results, like the rules of a game, you can then freely determine your own play. You can use the rules to win the game. The more abstract and objective the rule, the freer is the individual in the choice of his alternatives. The rules must be so written as to cover every possible eventuality of choice and action.

Applications

1. What is the primary subject, the subject that A. Delafield Smith wished to explore?
2. What is the analogous subject, the subject that Smith used to explore his primary subject?
3. Construct two parallel lists (like those on page 46), indicating the similarities that Smith finds between "rules" in a game and "laws" in society.
4. Indicate the major classifications, or "areas of resemblance," that Smith uses to structure his analogy.

Writing Projects

A. Below are two lists. Choose a subject from the left-hand column as your primary subject, and then explore it in terms of an analogous subject chosen from the right-hand column. Try not to stray from reality as you draw your analogy. Don't force parallels that distort the subject or that strike you as "fakey." (If you prefer, ignore the lists and compose your own exploratory analogy.)

body	masturbation
T.V.	ocean
mind	deformity
factory	blindness
making love	insanity
growing old	anthill
routine	torture
poverty	cancer
book	clothing
self-righteousness	ax
snobbery	sleeping pill

B. Write a four- to five-hundred-word essay based on your prewriting by analogy.

three

prewriting by brainstorming

Principle

Most people don't have a very high opinion of brainstorms, unless they're their own. Like the flash of lightning in a storm, brilliant but brief, the burst of insight in the mind that we call a brainstorm often lacks staying power.

United Press Photo

55

Folger Shakespeare Library

But the prewriting strategy of brainstorming* is a bit different. It's a strategy for "storming" the brain in the sense that we speak of an army "storming" a walled city in order to overrun its defenders and get at the riches within. It's an inductive approach, like the one Jack Webb uses in "Dragnet '70" when, in the role of Sergeant Joe Friday, he demands: "Just the facts, ma'am. All I want are the facts." Sooner or later he will have to try to make some sense out of the facts, and draw some conclusions from them. But to begin with, he just wants the facts.

Prewriting by brainstorming is a five-step process which allows you to:

1. recognize the richness and diversity of your subject (exploration)
2. decide on the particular aspect of your subject that you wish to investigate (limitation)
3. gather as much information as possible about this aspect (discovery)
4. make some sense out of the body of information you've assembled (classification)

---

* I've taken some liberties with the term "brainstorming," which typically refers to a *group* think-in. But it's the technique itself that's important, not the number of participants. As used in this chapter, then, "brainstorming" refers to the prewriting strategy, whether employed by an individual or by a group.

5. determine what you want to say to the reader, and the order in which you want to say it (selecting and ordering).

I · Exploration Through Brainstorming

As always, you should choose a subject that you are knowledgeable about—teachers, classes, roommates, dating, cars, light shows, family, and so forth. In order to explore your subject through brainstorming, you ask as many *questions* about your subject as you can think of. To illustrate this procedure let's take as our first example the subject "family," since all of us are familiar with it. Here are some of the questions we might ask that would lead us to recognize the breadth and complexity of this subject:

1. What are the functions of the family?
2. Are there significant differences between the urban family today and the rural family of the last century?
3. What does the present divorce rate suggest about family stability?
4. Does family life appeal to most young people today?
5. Why does family life appeal to me?
6. What are the advantages of family life?
7. What is a family? Is a commune of unmarried people a family? Are two unmarried people living together a family? Does a family imply having children?
8. Is the traditional concept of the family outmoded today?
9. How does a young person break free from his family?
10. What are some viable alternatives to the traditional family?

Notice that as I brainstormed the subject "family," I started out with some pretty conventional and not too interesting questions that came readily to mind. Then things got tougher and slower. But as I searched for additional questions, the questions began to probe more deeply and to become more intriguing and "real." This sort of progression from the facile and dull to the difficult and interesting is typical in the exploration stage of prewriting by brainstorming. Force yourself to go beyond the quick and easy questions. Keep probing. You will often find that the questions in the second half of your list are the ones that most need answering, and that require the deepest thought.

II · Limitation

The second step in prewriting by brainstorming is to limit yourself to one question about your subject or to a group of related questions that can be rephrased as one question. Even though I am a married man, I have serious doubts about the purpose, function, meaning, and rationale of the traditional family in a society such as ours. Therefore, I would like to limit the subject to the question, "Is the traditional concept of the family outmoded today?" When you limit your subject, choose the question or group of questions that interests you most.

III · Discovery

In the third stage of prewriting by brainstorming, you brainstorm for answers to the question you have asked. In this stage you should not content yourself with simple "either—or" answers or "yes and no" answers. Instead, you should seek to come up with as many answers as possible, and to make your answers as varied as possible, in order to take into account the complexity and ambiguity of the question you have raised.

■ Now, at this point something has occurred that would lead most authors to go back and revise what they've already written. But instead of doing that, I want to indicate to you what has happened because it bears on your own writing difficulties.

When I tried to brainstorm the question, "Is the traditional concept of the family outmoded today?," I couldn't make any progress. Nothing occurred to me. After about fifteen minutes of unproductive effort, I realized that answering the question meaningfully would require a fund of information and knowledge that I do not possess, and that, in addition, even a person who did possess such a fund of information and knowledge could not possibly answer the question in the restricted space of a four- to five-hundred-word essay. In short, in trying to answer this question I was violating the cardinal principle of responsible and effective writing: "Know your subject."

After realizing this, I had several alternatives:

1. I could go ahead with the question and try to fake my answers.
2. I could select another question from the list of questions about "family" and try to brainstorm for answers to that question.
3. I could choose a new subject and start over.

The only unacceptable alternative is 1, faking it. Alternatives 2 and 3 are equally responsible choices. Question 5 in the list on page 57 could be readily brainstormed, since it only requires knowledge of (or the ability to discover) one's own feelings, not the specialized sociological knowledge demanded by question 8. But by now you may be getting a bit weary of our original subject, and I know I am. So let's start over, using the subject "my roommate." You can draw on your current experience, and I can draw on some not so pleasant memories. ■

I · Exploration Through Brainstorming

1. What is my roommate's background?
2. What does my roommate look like?
3. What are some of the things my roommate and I do together?
4. What is my roommate's personality like?
5. What are my roommate's interests?
6. Why do I dislike my roommate?

II · Limitation

Question 6, "Why do I dislike my roommate?," interests me most, since I had a series of roommates when I was an undergraduate and graduate student, two of whom I despised.

III · Discovery

As noted earlier, the purpose of this stage is to brainstorm for as many answers to your question as possible. If your roommate is a real slob, you might come up with a list like this:

1. He's dirty.
2. He doesn't bathe very often.
3. His feet smell.
4. His dirty clothes smell.
5. He leaves his clothes all around the room.
6. He leaves his books lying around and scatters his things and never picks up after himself.
7. He doesn't help me clean the room.
8. He's inconsiderate.
9. He doesn't do his share of the work.
10. He's noisy and plays his record player when I'm trying to study, or turns on his TV, or talks loud on the phone.
11. He'll come in at night, drunk and boisterous, and bang around without any consideration for me.
12. He'll wake me up without realizing that I have to get up for an early class.
13. He's lazy; he oversleeps.
14. He's always having people into the room for bull sessions, even when I have an exam the next day.
15. He gets on my nerves and makes me mad.
16. He's dumb.
17. He's a big mouth.
18. He never seems to study.
19. He makes failing grades.
20. He brags about his conquests all the time, and about all the girls he's dated.

IV · Classification

After you brainstormed some answers to your question, you'll have lots of ideas but little or no structuring or grouping. So you should establish the major classifications, much like sorting a shuffled deck of cards into suits: clubs, diamonds, hearts, and spades. If you like, you can look at this process as *analyzing* your brainstorm. In other words, you determine the major points of view represented by your answers, and group your answers under these points of view. To do this, you should put a classification word to the right of each answer:

ANSWER	CLASSIFICATION
1. He's dirty.	Dirty
2. He doesn't bathe very often.	Dirty
3. His feet smell.	Dirty
4. His clothes smell.	Dirty
5. He leaves his clothes all around the room.	Inconsiderate
6. He leaves his books lying around and scatters his things and never picks up after himself.	Inconsiderate
7. He doesn't help me clean the room.	Inconsiderate
8. He's inconsiderate.	Inconsiderate
9. He doesn't do his share of the work.	Inconsiderate
10. He's noisy and plays his record player when I'm trying to study, or turns on his TV, or talks loud on the phone.	Inconsiderate
11. He'll come in late at night, drunk and boisterous, and bang around without any consideration for me.	Inconsiderate
12. He'll wake me up without realizing that I have to get up for an early class.	Inconsiderate
13. He's lazy; he oversleeps.	Lazy
14. He's always having people into the room for bull sessions, even when I have an exam the next day.	Inconsiderate
15. He gets on my nerves and makes me mad.	Effect on me
16. He's dumb.	Dumb
17. He's a big mouth.	Big mouth
18. He never seems to study.	Study habits
19. He makes failing grades.	Grades
20. He brags about his conquests all the time, and about all the girls he's dated.	Big mouth

V · Selecting and Ordering

A. Selecting

Some of the statements in the list above are really not answers to the question "Why do I dislike my roommate?" Statement 15, for example, is a result, not a cause; and statement 19 is an item of information about the subject "my roommate" rather than a direct answer to the question asked. Such irrelevant items should be scratched out.

Answers that are identified by a classification word which appears only once (or in some cases twice), such as statements 16 and 18, can be also scratched out. We can achieve a tighter focus by concentrating on the major classifications.

In the "roommate" example, then, we are left with three major points of view: dirty, inconsiderate, and big mouth. Our problem now is to order the items in each classification in an effective manner.

B. Ordering

When you order or structure your answers into a preliminary outline, you should (1) identify the major classifications with Roman numerals, (2) indicate points of view that are subdivisions of the major classifications with capital letters, and (3) identify aspects of a particular capital-letter point of view with arabic numerals.

In our example, I dislike my roommate because he is a dirty, inconsiderate big mouth. These three major characteristics can be identified with Roman numerals, and the rest of the outline can be organized under them. Hence, revising the order to save the roommate's most repulsive characteristic for last, we might come up with an outline like this:

WHY I DISLIKE MY ROOMMATE

I. He's a big mouth.
   A. He brags about how many girls he's made.
   B. In a discussion he always claims to know all about the subject, whatever it is.

c. In an argument, he shouts down anyone who disagrees with him.

II. He's inconsiderate.
    A. He doesn't do his share of the work.
        1. He never helps clean the room.
    B. He never picks up after himself.
        1. He leaves his clothes scattered around.
        2. He leaves his books and papers wherever he happens to drop them.
    c. He's noisy.
        1. He plays his record player and shouts into the phone when I'm trying to study.
        2. He comes in late at night, drunkenly boisterous, and bangs around with no consideration for me.
        3. He's always having people into the room for a bull session, even when he knows I have an exam the next day.

III. He's dirty.
    A. He doesn't bathe or shower more than once a week, and sometimes not even that often.
        1. His feet smell.
        2. His armpits smell.
        3. He reeks with stale sweat and other body odors.
    B. He wears the same clothes day after day.
        1. His shirts smell.
        2. His socks are rank.
        3. His undershorts are stained and foul.

NOTE: The outline above is considerably more refined than the raw list which emerged from brainstorming answers to the question. This illustrates that no step in the prewriting process is passive. In each step you refine, polish, and focus.

As you order your answers and classifications in outline form, you should search for additional reasons and examples that will make your point more convincing and vivid. You will find that you can rephrase and modify statements in the list to more accurately convey your meaning, and that some items, even though relevant, can be profitably omitted.

Formulating Your Thesis

After structuring your "brainstorm" in outline form, you are ready to formulate your thesis statement. Once again I will emphasize the importance of formulating the thesis *after* completing the prewriting process. In this case the thesis might read: "My roommate is a big mouth. He is inconsiderate. And he is the filthiest person I've ever known. I can't stand him."

Supplying the Specifics

As always, when you write your essay you should flesh out the bare bones of your outline with clarifying reasons, explanations, details, illustrations, examples, and so forth.

Process and Production

Student Process and Production

The student whose prewriting activities and essay appear below chose "teachers" as his general subject.

I · Exploration

His first step was to explore his subject in order to recognize its richness, complexity, and diversity, and in order to find a limited aspect which particularly interested him. To explore his general subject, he asked as many questions about it as he could think of:

1. What kind of people become teachers?
2. What kind of a job is teaching?
3. How do teachers spend their time outside of school?
4. What makes a person decide to become a teacher?
5. What makes a good teacher?
6. What makes a bad teacher?
7. What do I dislike most of all in teachers?
8. What do I like most of all in teachers?
9. What do students think of teachers?
10. How many students admire their teachers?
11. How many students want to become teachers?
12. What are the differences among teachers in primary schools, teachers in secondary schools, and teachers in colleges and universities?
13. What effects do teachers have on their students' values?
14. Do teachers of different subjects have different types of personalities?

15. Are teachers most motivated by job security, or by a desire to inspire their students, or what?
16. How do some adults whom I know regard teachers? In other words, are teachers respected in our society or not?

II · Limitation

The student decided that questions 6 and 7 interested him most, and that he could draw on his extensive personal experience as a student to answer them. He rephrased them as a single question: "What characteristics in teachers do I dislike?"

III · Discovery

When the student brainstormed for answers to his question, he came up with these:

1. I dislike teachers who are unprepared for their classes.
2. I dislike teachers who don't know their subject.
3. Then there are droning teachers, teachers who are monotonous and boring.
4. Some teachers have shrill or rasping voices.
5. Some teachers speak so fast that you can't take notes.
6. I dislike disorganized teachers, for all you get is a big jumble.
7. Some teachers have bad personal habits or distracting mannerisms.
8. Some teachers are rigid and dogmatic; they don't accept any points of view that are different from their own.
9. I dislike teachers who are aloof and distant; they seem to be detached from their students.
10. I dislike teachers who are too personal; they want to get involved with their students personally and find out everything about their lives. It's a kind of prying.
11. I dislike teachers who have "pets," who show favoritism by giving certain students special consideration and privileges.
12. Some teachers let their students walk all over them and don't maintain any order or discipline in the classroom, so nobody can learn anything.
13. Some teachers don't have any sense of style; they don't know how to dress.

14. I dislike teachers who assign busy work instead of important assignments; they make students spend a lot of time doing meaningless exercises.
15. I dislike teachers who are too tough, too harsh. They give assignments that are unreasonably long or make assignments without giving students enough time to complete them.
16. I dislike teachers who assign readings that the student can't understand or that don't mean anything to him. Such teachers don't consider the needs and interests of the student, what kinds of things *he* might want to learn.
17. I dislike teachers who are moody and inconsistent, who come to class one day prepared and good-humored and the next day come in unprepared and ill-tempered.

IV · Classification

The student has discovered numerous characteristics he dislikes in teachers. His job now is to group these characteristics into some major classes so that he can present them in an orderly and systematic fashion. If he started writing at this point, he would simply produce a jumbled, rambling, undifferentiated list. Hence, his next step was to analyze his list of answers in order to determine the major types of characteristics that he dislikes in teachers.

CHARACTERISTIC	CLASSIFICATION
1. I dislike teachers who are unprepared for their classes.	Preparation
2. I dislike teachers who don't know their subject.	Knowledge of subject
3. Then there are droning teachers, teachers who are monotonous and boring.	Speech
4. Some teachers have shrill or rasping voices.	Speech
5. Some teachers speak so fast that you can't take notes.	Speech
6. I dislike disorganized teachers, for all you get is a big jumble.	Preparation

CHARACTERISTIC	CLASSIFICATION
7. Some teachers have bad personal habits or distracting mannerisms.	Personal traits
8. Some teachers are rigid and dogmatic; they don't accept any points of view that are different from their own.	Personality
9. I dislike teachers who are aloof and distant; they seem to be detached from their students.	Personality
10. I dislike teachers who are too personal; they want to get involved with their students personally and find out everything about their lives. It's a kind of prying.	Personality
11. I dislike teachers who have pets, who show favoritism by giving certain students special consideration and privileges.	Favoritism
12. Some teachers let their students walk all over them and don't maintain any order or discipline in the classroom, so nobody can learn anything.	Order
13. Some teachers don't have any sense of style; they don't know how to dress.	Personal traits
14. I dislike teachers who assign busy work instead of important assignments; they make students spend a lot of time doing meaningless exercises.	Assignments
15. I dislike teachers who are too tough, too harsh. They give assignments that are unreasonably long or make assignments without giving students enough time to complete them.	Assignments
16. I dislike teachers who assign readings that the student can't understand or that don't mean anything to him. Such teachers don't consider the needs and interests of the student, what kinds of things *he* might want to learn.	Assignments

17. I dislike teachers who are moody and   Personality
inconsistent, who come to class one day
prepared and good-humored and the
next day come in unprepared and
ill-tempered.

V · Selecting and Ordering

A. Selecting

The characteristics that the student dislikes in teachers fall into five major classes:

preparation (2)
speech (3)
personal traits (2)
personality (4)
assignments (3)

The student decided to limit his discussion to the three classifications that appeared most often: speech, personality, and assignments.

B. Ordering

The student next ordered his findings in outline form in order to plan the overall structure and form of his essay.

CHARACTERISTICS THAT I DISLIKE IN TEACHERS

  I. I dislike teachers who are dogmatic or aloof or too personal.
   A. Some teachers are rigid and dogmatic.
      1. They don't accept points of view different from their own.
      2. They don't allow free discussion of ideas in the classroom.
      3. They present only one side of an issue.
   B. A teacher may also be too aloof and distant.
      1. Such a teacher seems detached from his students.
      2. It's hard to like him or to work hard for him because you feel he doesn't care about you as a person.

    c. On the other hand, a teacher may be too personal.

        1. Such a teacher doesn't respect the student's right to privacy.

        2. Such a teacher, like Miss Jean Brodie in the movie *The Prime of Miss Jean Brodie,* tries to pry into and get involved in the student's private life.

II. Some teachers don't know how to speak effectively in class.

    A. Some drone on in a boring monotone.

        1. They don't vary the rate or pitch of their voice.

        2. They make even interesting subjects seem dull and lifeless.

    B. Others have shrill or rasping voices that grate on your nerves. When they speak, their voices are like the screech of chalk on the blackboard.

    c. Still others talk so fast that it's impossible to take notes.

        1. If you try to take notes, you quickly get behind and lose track of what they're saying.

        2. But if you don't take notes, you can't review the material they covered at exam time.

        3. So, either way, you've had it.

III. I don't like teachers who have personality traits and speech habits like those I've mentioned—but I can at least tolerate them. Teachers who make meaningless or unreasonably harsh assignments are the ones I really hate.

    A. Some teachers make meaningless busy-work assignments.

        1. They may insist that you copy out each word in a long spelling list five or even ten times.

        2. They may give you a long passage and tell you to label each part of speech as a "grammar exercise."

        3. If you already know how to spell the word you're copying or if you already know how to identify parts of speech, these assignments are a waste of time.

    B. Teachers sometimes make unreasonably difficult assignments.

        1. The assignment may be one that takes a lot of time, like doing a research paper, but the teacher makes it due in two or three days.

        2. The assignment may be so difficult that no matter how hard the student tries, he can't do a good job.

NOTE: As the student developed his outline, he added additional ideas, reasons, and examples in support of his three main points. Notice too, as you read the essay written from the outline, how the student adds even more specific illustrations, and how he makes smooth transitions from point to point.

Characteristics That I Dislike in Teachers

Paintings and written descriptions of hell have always struck me as more convincing and arresting than similar visual or written impressions of heaven. Many people I've talked to who regularly go to the Indianapolis 500 admit to hoping that a spectacular crash will relieve the monotony of the cars circling the track. In short, the painful and unpleasant seem to hold more attraction and to arouse more interest than their opposites. Though most of the teachers I have had have been competent and a few even inspiring, I find myself drawn to describe characteristics of those I haven't liked. Some of these were dogmatic or aloof or pryingly personal. Others were unable to speak effectively. And some, the ones I found myself truly hating, habitually made meaningless or unreasonably harsh assignments.

Some teachers have personalities that make them dogmatic or aloof or excessively personal. The rigidly dogmatic teacher is unable to accept points of view that differ from his own. If he supports Nixon's foreign policy, he will not allow students to criticize it. Such a teacher stifles free discussion of ideas in the classroom. He presents only one side of an issue and does not allow the students to discuss other sides of it. Another personality trait that I dislike in teachers is aloofness or distance. Aloof teachers seem to be detached from their students. They tend to be extremely formal and reserved in the classroom. It's hard for a student to do work for such a teacher, because he feels that the teacher doesn't care about him as a person. On the other hand, a teacher may be too personal. Far from putting too great a distance between himself and the student, the overly personal teacher wants to get too close. He doesn't respect the student's right to privacy. Such a teacher, like Miss Jean Brodie in the movie *The Prime of Miss Jean Brodie,* tries to pry into and get involved in the student's private life.

Teachers who are unable to speak effectively are also annoying. Some drone on in a boring monotone. Since they don't vary the rate or pitch of their voice, they make even interesting subjects seem dull and lifeless. It's as if they themselves were virtually without energy or interest, and the drone of their voice creates a similarly lifeless atmosphere in the classroom. Other teachers have shrill or rasping voices that grate on one's nerves. When they speak, their voices are like the screech of chalk on a blackboard. Still others talk so fast that it is impossible to take notes. If you try to take notes you get behind or lose track of what they're saying, but if you don't take notes you can't review the material they covered when it is time to take an exam; so, either way, you've had it.

But the teachers I really hate are the ones who make meaningless or unusually harsh assignments. Teachers who make pointless busy-work assignments may, for example, insist that you copy out each word in a long spelling list five or even ten times. Or they may tell you, as a grammar exercise, to label each part of speech in a long passage. If you already know how to spell the words you're copying or if you already know how to identify parts of speech, these assignments are simply a waste of time. Yet, since they are "required," you have to do them no matter how angry or disgusted they may make you. And then, a student may get a teacher who makes unreasonably difficult assignments. The assignment may be one that takes a lot of time, like doing a research paper, but the teacher may make it due in two or three days. Another type of assignment may be difficult not because there is insufficient time allowed for its completion, but simply because it requires knowledge or abilities that the student doesn't have. When such an assignment is made, the student can't do a good job no matter how hard he tries.

Teachers with personality problems, teachers with bad speech habits, and teachers who make ill-considered assignments—these are the types of teachers I dislike. Unfortunately, teachers with qualities like these tend to make stronger and longer-lasting impressions than those who do their job well. Members of the teaching profession who would like to see that profession become more respected by both students and the general public would be well advised to consider ways of removing the black sheep from among them.

When an author has used prewriting by analysis or prewriting by analogy, the prewriting technique can generally be recognized in the completed essay. But there is no way to tell from a completed essay whether or not the writer has used brainstorming as his prewriting method; we can only guess. However, the essay that follows might well have grown out of a brainstorming session in which the central question was "What are the characteristics of Hippiebums?"

Hippiebums · Liza Williams

OK so you are wearing beads, and your hair is long and from the back you might be anyone, and from the front your face isn't too different either, your expression, is it an expression, is non-attendance, and your style is all I ever know of you. Style, it's all style and not much content, but what is the definition of decadence? Is it the substitution of style for content? Is that why so many love children smile a lot and score off you for everything they can get, cigarettes, hey man, lay a cigarette on me, or another ploy, anybody got a match? OK, now who's got a cigarette to go with it? Or you walk into an underground paper office where there is a big sign on the wall that says "Don't make magic, Be magic" and "Love" and you ask about something and receive cold indifference, they are too busy manufacturing love to give away any samples.

Hippiebums, dirty long-haired hippiebums with nowhere to go and nothing to do and they spend a lot of time using your daylight and your floor doing their nothing, so that if you have something to do it is impossible. Who's that bunch of hippies out there in our garage-way mending their shoes and dancing and inviting the man to come and bust us, while we stand at the window and worry, from inside our tenuous safety, where we just got through with a lot of

cleaning up after a departed hippie community, washing, wall paint-
ing, and removing piles of animal shit from under the refrigerator?

Split, that what it's come to, a big rift, hippies and hippiebums.
Upstairs the acid freaks are screaming and shouting and beating
each other up and chasing each other around in lace dresses and the
child who lives there sits at our table asking for food and wondering
where her mother is, only not too hopefully.

Hippiebums give you presents, like dirty feathers or one bead or
the clap. Hippiebums tell you about mystical experiences while they
finger your breadbox. Hippiebums start off on your floor and make
it to the couch and then eye your bed. When it gets tight for them
they split, but they let you keep the feather or bead or the clap as a
souvenir. You're materialistic they mumble at you as they drag
themselves out your door, their pockets stuffed with peanut butter
sandwiches.

Hippiebums write bad poetry and draw ugly pictures and make
you look at them. They sing dull songs to one chord change and tell
you how it is, letting you in on the secrets of life. Hippiebums hitch
rides with you and roll joints in the back seat leaving seeds on the
carpet. Hippiebums are just leaving for San Francisco or have just
come back. Hippiebums use your telephone to call Chicago or Great
Falls and three friends in New York; they pass the time on your
phone. Hippiebums are always there at mealtimes but can't wipe
dishes; hippiebums bring their friends over but never tell you their
names.

Hippiebums come from middle-class homes and want you to be
their parents, want you to pay their rent, want to make your world
their high school. Hippiebums believe in the abundance of the
Great Society, and want you to supply it. Hippiebums are predatory
but wear a disguise of love. Hippiebums serenade you with their
bells and dance for you, stepping on your feet.

I used to smile at everyone with a button or a bell or a flower, I
used to think how beautiful it was all becoming, how rich it was,
how sweet and good. But it's fantasy time, that's what it is, fantasy
time in the twentieth century and style is where it's at, and only a
few maintain content, and content, in the end, is really what creates
a good world, and love, and being together with people and doing
and making peace and feeling love and sustaining energy. So don't
feel bad if you can't love every long-haired flower-bell child in the
road; things aren't always what they seem.

A. Choose a subject you are knowledgeable about and perform the five steps in the "prewriting by brainstorming" process:

1. Exploration
2. Limitation
3. Discovery
4. Classification
5. Selecting and ordering

B. Write a four- to five-hundred-word essay based on the outline that emerged from your prewriting activities.

four

prewriting by systematic inquiry

Principle

Generally, when you use the prewriting strategies of analysis, analogy, and brainstorming, you will be dealing with subjects that your audience knows at least something about. Your reader may not know how to prepare a hit of speed, but he has some general knowledge about drugs and amphetamines. Your reader may not know in what ways *your* high school was like a jail, but he has some knowledge of the broad subject "high school." Your reader may not have met *your* roommate, but he knows what a roommate is, and has probably lived with one.

Prewriting by systematic inquiry, in contrast, is particularly useful when you wish to help your reader understand a subject about which he is presumed to be totally (or almost totally) ignorant. When *you* know what something is and wish to explain it fully to an audience that knows little or nothing about it, you can use the technique of prewriting by systematic inquiry.

This prewriting technique consists of asking yourself, and then stating the answers to, four questions:

1. What are the characteristics of my subject?   Characteristics
2. How does my subject differ from other
   similar subjects?   Differentia
3. What is the range of variation of my subject?   Range of variation
4. What is the context of my subject?   Context

If you wish to write about your subject from a historical standpoint—that is, if you wish to explain it not just as it is today but as it has developed and changed—then you need only add a "time" or "process" element to each of the questions above. Hence:

1. What were its characteristics when it first came into being and along the line of its development to its present form?
2. What made it different from similar things at its inception (or early in its development) and along the line of its development?
3. What was its range of variation at its inception and at various points along the line of its development?

4. What was its larger context at the point of its inception and along the line of its development?

Maybe this is beginning to sound complex and difficult, so let's get specific. Let's say you want to explain to your reader a stock market technique known as "short-selling" or "selling stocks short." Let's further suppose that you wish to regard the technique as *static;* that is, you're not interested in showing what its origins were or how it has developed over a period of time. Instead, you're simply interested in explaining the nature of this practice as it stands today. Your prewriting activity would consist of *systematic inquiry;* you would ask yourself, and then answer, each of the four questions we have listed.

Exploration Through Systematic Inquiry

QUESTION 1: What are the *characteristics* of short-selling? (What is it? How would one recognize it? How do you go about doing it?)

ANSWERS: It's a way to make money when a stock declines in market price.

You sell shares of stocks that you don't own.

You "borrow" shares and then sell them.

Eventually, you have to buy shares to repay those you borrowed.

QUESTION 2: How is it *different* from similar things? (How does it differ from other types of stock market transactions? What distinguishes it? What makes it unique?)

ANSWERS: Short-selling is designed to make money from a falling stock, whereas the usual procedure is to buy a stock in the hope that it will go up in value.

You are selling something you don't own, whereas when you buy stocks, they belong to you.

Theoretically, there is no limit to the amount of money you can lose on a short sale. When you buy stocks, your potential loss is limited to the amount you paid for the stock.

Short-selling is almost always speculative. A short sale is usually designed to achieve a quick profit. On the other hand, many people who buy stocks long (that is, who pay for them when they buy them, and hope they will increase in value) do so for investment purposes.

QUESTION 3: What is its *range of variation?* (What different types of short sales are there?)

ANSWERS: The most common type of short sale is the sale of borrowed stock in the expectation of being able to buy the stock at a lower price.

Another type of short sale is called "selling against the box." This procedure is designed to protect a profit on a stock one already owns.

QUESTION 4: What is the context of short-selling? (In what larger setting does it occur? How is it related to this larger setting or context?)

ANSWERS: Short-selling is one of a large number of relatively sophisticated stock market techniques designed to take advantage of special market situations.

Short-selling is a way for a trader to remain active when the market is falling, instead of sitting on the sidelines.

Explain, Illustrate, Clarify

When your subject is new and strange to your reader, it is essential that you help him toward an understanding of it by generous use of details, examples, and clarifying explanations. The answers to the four questions are only the bare bones of your essay. Their meaning may be clear to you, but you must put yourself in the place of your reader and ask yourself whether their meaning will be clear to him. When there's any chance that the reader may not understand, *clarify*.

Thus, if a reader who knows little or nothing about short-selling is to understand this stock market technique, the answers listed above must be fleshed out, as in the essay that follows:

Short-Selling

"Short-selling," or "selling stocks short," is a stock market technique that one can use to make a profit when a stock goes *down* in price.

The short-seller tells his broker to "sell short" a number of shares of a certain stock. The short-seller does not own the shares of stock that he directs his broker to sell. But this creates no immediate problem. His broker simply "borrows" the shares and then sells them on the stock market as if the short-seller actually owned them. Eventually, of course, the short-seller must buy as many shares of the stock as he sold short, in order to repay the broker the shares that the broker borrowed.

We can illustrate the process of the short sale with a hypothetical example. Say that shares of General Motors stock are selling at $50 per share on the market and that a person believes that, at this price, General Motors stock is overvalued. In other words, he be· lieves that the price of General Motors stock is too high and that it will decline. He could then "sell short" 100 shares of General Motors stock at $50 per share. For this sale he would receive the sum of $5,000, less commission charges and taxes. However, the short-seller would now owe his broker 100 shares of General Motors stock which, sooner or later, he would have to repay. If the price of General Motors stock did indeed decline, say to $25 per share, the short seller could "cover" his short sale. To cover a short sale is to purchase the number of shares necessary to repay the loan from one's broker. If our hypothetical short-seller covered his short sale by buying 100 shares of General Motors stock at $25 per share, he would make a profit of $2,500. He would make this profit because, though he sold the borrowed General Motors stock at $50 per share, it only cost him $25 per share to repay the loan.

The crucial difference between the short sale and the outright purchase of stocks is that the potential for loss on a short sale is, theoretically at least, unlimited. Returning to our General Motors example, there is theoretically no limit on how high the stock could go in market price. It could go to $100 or $200 or $300 per share over a period of time. Hence, there is theoretically no limit to the amount one could lose on a short sale. For example, if the short-seller finally decided to cover his short sale when General Motors stock was selling at $300 per share, 100 shares of General Motors stock would cost him $30,000—for a loss of $25,000. On the other hand, when one buys a stock outright, his potential loss is limited to the amount that the stock cost him. Thus, if one bought 100 shares of General Motors stock at $50, the price of the stock could decline no lower than $0; the loss would be limited to the purchase price of $5,000. Finally, short-selling is almost always speculative. Many people who buy stocks long do so for investment reasons. They base their purchase on an analysis of the worth and future profit potential of the company and intend to hold the stock for a relatively long period of time. But people who sell stock short almost always do so in the expectation of a relatively quick profit. They sell short not on the basis of the company's long-term profit potential, but on the basis of what they feel to be the stock's current market vulnerability.

The most common type of short sale is that which we have been describing: the short-seller sells borrowed stock in the hope of being able to buy the stock at a lower price. Another form of short-selling is known as "selling short against the box." This procedure is designed to protect one's gain on a stock that he owns. Say, using our General Motors example, that one has bought 100 shares of General Motors stock at $30 per share and the stock rises to $50. At this point the owner of the stock has a potential profit of $2,000 on the 100 shares. In other words, he paid $3,000 for the stock, and he can now sell it for $5,000. In order to protect that profit, the investor might "sell short against the box" 100 shares of General Motors stock. From this sale he would realize $5,000. He can now, at any time, repay the loan involved in the short sale with the 100 shares of General Motors stock bought at $30 and have a net profit of $2,000, less various commission charges and taxes. If, however, the market price of General Motors stock now *declines,* the investor protects his profit because, for every dollar he loses on the stock owned outright, he makes a dollar on the stock sold short.

Short-selling is but one of a large number of relatively sophisticated techniques that have been developed by people wishing to take advantage of special stock market situations. It allows a trader to make money, or at least attempt to make money, when a stock is declining in price, not just when it is rising. Thus, short-selling is a way for a trader to remain active when the market or a stock is falling, instead of merely sitting on the sidelines. It is a trader's device for making hay not only while the sun shines but also while the rain falls.

NOTE: When you use systematic inquiry as the basis for prewriting, you should always decide in advance how fully you are going to treat your subject. Are you going to explain it in one page, three pages, twenty pages, or five hundred? Although the prewriting technique directs and orders your investigation and presentation, it does not put any limits on the scope or breadth of that investigation and presentation.

If you do not feel that you can adequately explain the characteristics, differentia, range of variation, and context of your subject in the space and time available to you, you should use another prewriting strategy, such as analysis, to discover a limited aspect of your subject that can be fully explained in the time and space available.

Process and Production

Student Process and Production

The student whose prewriting activities and essay appear below wished to explain to his reader the nature of hot-air balloons.

Exploration Through Systematic Inquiry

The student's first step was to explore his subject by supplying detailed answers to the four questions that we have discussed.

QUESTION 1: What are the *characteristics* of hot-air balloons? (What are they? How would one recognize a hot-air balloon?)

ANSWERS: The balloon consists of an envelope of nylon, usually about fifty feet in diameter.

At the top of the balloon, there is a "spill flap" that will instantaneously release the hot air in the balloon.

Below the balloon and attached to it is a gondola, made either of wicker or of aluminum.

Attached to the gondola is some sort of heat source, usually a propane burner.

QUESTION 2: How are hot-air balloons *different* from similar things? (How do hot-air balloons differ from other types of balloons? What distinguishes them and makes them unique?)

ANSWERS: The hot-air balloon is substantially different from the two other major vehicles for lighter-than-air-flight—the dirigible and the blimp.

Unlike both dirigible and blimp, the hot-air balloon is not filled with gas.

Unlike both dirigibles and blimps, hot-air balloons carry no motor, so they cannot be directed or "steered."

QUESTION 3: What is the *range of variation* of hot-air balloons? (What different types of hot-air balloons are there?)

ANSWERS: Hot-air balloons come in a large variety of sizes. They range from 40 feet in diameter, which would be a one-man balloon, up to six-man balloons with a diameter of 65 feet and a capacity of 120,000 cubic feet of hot air.

The largest hot-air balloons ever made had a capacity of approximately 800,000 cubic feet. These mammoth hot-air balloons were used by showmen of the 1800s and early 1900s.

The most common use of hot-air balloons today is for what is called "sport ballooning." A person just takes off for fun and a car follows him.

There are also racing versions of hot-air balloons. The racing balloon has a smaller and lighter gondola than a sport balloon. Finally, there is a range of variation in the material used for the gondola. The British tend to prefer wicker gondolas because they have a lot of bounce. American companies tend to prefer aluminum gondolas.

QUESTION 4: What is the *context* of hot-air balloons? (In what larger setting do hot-air balloons occur? How are hot-air balloons related to this larger setting or context?)

ANSWERS: The hot-air balloon is one of a relatively small variety of vehicles that man has devised to work with, rather than against, nature.

The hot-air balloon, like the glider and the sailboat, depends on natural rather than man-made forces.

Like the glider and the sailboat, the hot-air balloon is a silent vehicle.

Ultimately, the appeal of the hot-air balloon, like the appeal of the sailboat and the glider, lies in the fact that it allows man to cooperate with nature rather than oppose her with man-made engines of force and power.

Writing the Essay

Notice that in the completed essay below, the "answers" to the four questions are explained, illustrated, and clarified. Notice, too, that the student does not include in his essay all the answers that he wrote down during the prewriting stage.

Hot-Air Balloons

The hot-air balloon gets its name from its source of buoyancy, which is, quite literally, "hot air." The balloon bag, or "envelope," is made of nylon and, when inflated, resembles an inverted pear. At the top of the balloon is a "spill flap" which, when opened, instantaneously releases the hot air in the balloon. Attached to the bottom of the balloon, as to the narrow part of an inverted pear, is a gondola in which the balloonist or balloonists ride. The gondola is a sort of "basket," constructed either of wicker or aluminum. Attached to this gondola, above the heads of the balloonist and directly below the narrow opening in the balloon envelope, is the heat source, the source of the hot air. In most hot-air balloons used today, this heat source consists of a propane burner similar to that used in camp-stoves, but much larger.

Although the hot-air balloon is a vehicle for lighter-than-air flight, it is substantially different from the two other major vehicles for such flight, the dirigible and the blimp. Both the dirigible and the blimp use lighter-than-air gas, either helium or the highly explosive hydrogen, for their buoyancy. And both have motors, which means that, unlike the hot-air balloon, they can be directed or "steered." In the hot-air balloon you "drift" rather than "direct."

Although distinctly different from the dirigible and the blimp, the hot-air balloon shares the range of variation that characterizes these other lighter-than-air craft. It varies in size and in the use to which it is put. A one-man hot-air balloon may be no more than 40 feet in diameter, while a six-man hot-air balloon, the largest available commercially, will often have a diameter of 65 feet. Similarly, there are a number of uses for the hot-air balloon. The most common use is for what is called "sport ballooning." The sport balloonist is an aficionado who enjoys the thrill of the take-off, the serenity of the drifting, and the excitement of the always unpredictable landing. But the popularity of "racing" in hot-air balloons is growing. The racing hot-air balloon is a stripped-down version of the sport balloon. Weight is saved wherever possible, especially in the gondola—which, in the racing balloon, may be no more than a lacy webbing enveloping the balloonist.

But whatever its size or purpose, the hot-air balloon is special. It is one of a relatively small variety of vehicles that man has devised to work with, rather than against, nature. Like the glider and the sailboat, the hot-air balloon depends on natural rather than man-made forces. Like both glider and sailboat, the hot-air balloon is a silent vehicle. Ultimately, then, the appeal of all three vehicles lies in the fact that they allow man to cooperate with nature rather than oppose her with man-made engines of force and violence.

Professional Production

Like the other prewriting strategies we have discussed, prewriting by systematic inquiry is used by professional writers. The author of the following essay uses the four-step process of systematic inquiry to order his explanation of "cultural anthropology." As you read the essay, see if you can recognize each of the four steps, and the points at which the author moves from one step to another.

Cultural Anthropology · Ashley Montagu

Cultural anthropology is concerned with the study of man's cultures. By "culture" the anthropologist understands what may be called the man-made part of the environment: the pots and pans, the laws and institutions, the art, religion, philosophy. Whatever a particular group of people living together as a functioning population have learned to do as human beings, their way of life, in short, is to be regarded as culture. The cultural anthropologist studies different cultures and compares them with one another in order to learn how it is that people come to do what they do in so many different ways, and also to learn, wherever possible, the relationships of one culture to another. He tries to find those common elements in all cultures which can be summarized in terms of generalizations or laws which are true of all cultures. Where there are differences, he tries to find the causes of these differences.

The cultural anthropologist is interested in all the forms that human social behavior assumes in organized societies. He cannot remain contented with the mere description of these forms, for he desires to understand how they have come into being, and so the cultural anthropologist must often be quite as good a psychologist as he is anything else. Fundamentally what he is really interested in is the nature of human nature. Today there is quite a flourishing school of anthropologists known as the personality-in-culture school. These cultural anthropologists, such as Margaret Mead, Clyde Kluckhohn, John Honigmann, Francis Hsu, and many others, are interested in tracing the relationship of the cultures in which human beings are socialized, that is, brought up, to the kind of personalities they develop.

Other cultural anthropologists are interested as specialists in studying such aspects of the cultures of different peoples as their legal institutions, social organization, religion, mythology, language, and their material culture such as their art, pottery, basketry, implements, and the like. Some cultural anthropologists take whole tribes for their special study and spend from many months to many years attempting to study every aspect of their culture.

Traditionally the cultural anthropologist has studied the so-called "primitive peoples" of this earth, and the major part of the anthropologist's attention still continues to be devoted to the cultures of such peoples, but in more recent years anthropologists have been turning their attention to the study of the technologically more advanced peoples of the earth. Today we have good anthropological studies not only of the Australian aborigines and the Congo pygmies, but also of the Japanese, the Chinese, the Germans, the Americans, the English, the Norwegians, and many others.

Formerly the study of modern societies was left to the sociologist (sociology = the study of society). Today the methods of the cultural anthropologist have greatly influenced those of the sociologist, but the difference between the two disciplines remains; the sociologist studies modern societies in great detail; the anthropologist brings to the study of the modern societies a method which is at once wider and deeper than that of the sociologist.

Today there are specialists who are known as *applied* anthropologists. These are essentially cultural anthropologists who bring their special methods to bear principally upon the problems of industry. They go into a plant and study the relationships between the workers and their employers, between the worker and his work, and they advise on the methods of improving these relationships.

There are cultural anthropologists who work in hospitals in collaboration with psychiatrists. They study the relationships within the hospital between patient and doctor, administration and staff, and they conduct collaborative studies of whole districts in order to throw light upon the genesis of mental illness and its possible prevention.

The collaboration between anthropologists and psychiatrists in the study of the cultures of different societies has been very fruitful indeed, and holds much promise for the future.

Another branch of cultural anthropology is *archaeology* (often unkindly called the moldier part of anthropology). Archaeology is the science which studies cultures that no longer exist, basing its findings on the study of cultural products and subsistence remains uncovered by excavation and similar means. If anthropologists are "the glamour boys" of the social sciences, archaeologists are "the glamour boys" of anthropology. All of which means that their specialty can be a very exciting one indeed, even though it generally entails a great deal of hard work, with far too much sand in one's hair, one's boots, and one's dried-out sandwiches. What the archaeologist is interested in doing is not merely to disinter an extinct culture, but to trace its relationships to other cultures. In this way archaeologists have been able to solve many problems which would otherwise have remained puzzling and to link up cultures which in their present form hardly seem related.

.   .   .

The anthropologist is first and foremost interested in human beings, no matter what the shape of their heads, the color of their skin, or the form of their noses. As a scientist he is interested in the facts about human beings, and as an anthropologist he knows that the facts are vastly more interesting than the fancies, the false beliefs, and the downright distortions of the facts, which some misguided persons seem always to have found it necessary to perpetrate. Humanity has a wonderfully interesting history, and it is the principal function of the anthropologist to reveal that history to the student as simply and as clearly as possible. . . .

Applications

Indicate the following divisions in the essay:

1. Discussion of the general *characteristics* of cultural anthropology.
2. *Differentia:* discussion of how cultural anthropology differs from a similar discipline.
3. Discussion of the *range of variation* of cultural anthropology.
4. Discussion of the larger *context,* which gives us an overview of the subject and enables us to see the relation of cultural anthropology to a broader system or pattern.

Writing Projects

A. Practice prewriting by systematic inquiry on a subject that is probably unfamiliar to most of your fellow students. If nothing occurs to you, you can choose one of the subjects listed below. As you list answers to each of the four questions in this prewriting process, plan for a two- to four-page essay on the subject.

Shill	Harlequin
Samovar	Flying buttress
Roman à clef	Ontology
Aardwolf	Claque
Angiosperm	Gharry
Atavist	Gnu
Galapagos Islands	Apteryx
Zymurgy	Vicuña
Ombudsman	Bouillabaisse
Paisley	Ragout
Dalmation Coast	Anisette
Mugwump	Lapis lazuli

B. Write a two- to four-page essay based on your prewriting activities. In writing your essay, follow this order: (1) characteristics, (2) differences from similar things, (3) range of variation, (4) context.

About the Author

Ray Kytle, Assistant Professor of English and Director of Composition at Central Michigan University, received his B.A. degree from the University of Oklahoma and his M.A. from Southern Illinois University. He is consulting editor in freshman and sophomore literature, language, and composition for a major textbook publisher and is a contributor to *College Composition and Communication*. Other books written or edited by Professor Kytle and published by Random House are *Confrontation: Issues of the 70s, Clear Thinking for Composition,* and *Composition: Discovery and Communication.*